THE HIGHLANDS
LAND & LIGHT

CRAIG AITCHISON

THE HIGHLANDS
LAND & LIGHT

CRAIG AITCHISON

F

FRANCES LINCOLN LIMITED
PUBLISHERS

For Alison

Frances Lincoln Limited
4 Torriano Mews
Torriano Avenue
London NW5 2RZ
www.franceslincoln.com

The Highlands: Land and Light
Copyright © Frances Lincoln Limited 2012
Text and photographs copyright © Craig Aitchison 2012
 First Frances Lincoln edition 2012

A catalogue record for this book is available from
the British Library.

ISBN 978-0-7112-3274-7

Printed and bound in China

9 8 7 6 5 4 3 2 1

Page 1: Loch Hourn, Knoydart.
Pages 2 and 3: Achnahaird Bay,
Sutherland.
Pages 4 and 5: The Cobbler, Argyll
and Bute.

CONTENTS

Sgùrr an Fhidhleir, Coigach.

INTRODUCTION

It is the contrast that draws me to the wild places of Scotland. Living and working as I do amid the urban ubiquity of Scotland's Central belt, it is heartening to know that a few hours' travelling can take me to a wilderness of desolate beauty unsurpassed anywhere in the world. There, the relentless pace and pressures of twenty-first-century life give way to a primeval sense of peace and freedom in an environment where the passage of time can be measured in geological ages rather than working days.

Scotland's landscape has long been celebrated. Its rich natural heritage and incredible geodiversity are unusual for a country of its size. The white beaches of the Hebrides give way to the jagged peaks of the west coast while the broad, glaciated Cairngorm plateau gives rise to the east. This spectacular drama is played out amid continually changing light, thanks to Scotland's notoriously volatile weather, which constantly transforms the landscape and ensures that no two moments are ever truly the same. The Highlands (broadly speaking the area north of the Highland Boundary Fault, which crosses Scotland from Helensburgh to Stonehaven) are therefore a photographer's paradise. In this book I endeavour to capture not just the manifestation of that landscape but also the feelings that it inspires.

Scotland's varied landscape is the result of a remarkable geological journey that started hundreds of millions of years ago in the southern hemisphere. Drifting slowly northwards, the landmass has moved through all of the Earth's climatic zones from polar to tropical. In the process, tectonic plate movement, volcanic activity and ice ages have all left their individual mark on the landscape, creating many of the distinctive mountain ranges and landmarks with which we are familiar today. Scotland is not just a single landmass but is, in fact, composed of separate pieces of the Earth's crust that fused together in the distant past.

This remarkable geological jigsaw can be seen in the unique variety of rock found throughout the country, from relatively young sandstone formations all the way to the Lewisian Gniess of the north-west, at approximately three billion years old some of the oldest rock that can be found anywhere on Earth. Numerous world-famous geological features such as the 'unconformities' at Siccar Point in Berwickshire discovered by James Hutton in 1788 have also led to ground-breaking discoveries about the age of the planet itself. When considering the elemental forces that created this land it is difficult to imagine that human habitation could have significantly changed it. In fact, however, the presence of man has had a dramatic, often pervasive, influence on our landscape.

Archaeological studies have uncovered evidence of human habitation in Scotland dating back to prehistoric times. The well-preserved settlement at Skara Brae in Orkney, for instance, was inhabited as long ago as 3200 BC and it is known that people lived in Scotland several thousand years before that. The earliest Scots were hunter-gatherers whose survival depended on catching and killing wild animals. As early farming practices began to emerge, parts of the extensive forests that dominated much of the Scottish landscape began to disappear to make way for crops and farm animals. This was the start of a human-driven process of deforestation that contributed significantly to the decimation of the once mighty Caledonian Pine forests – to the point that just 1 per cent of the original woodland remains. Much of this now lies in protected areas but the damage has long since been done, a permanent reminder of the influence that human habitation has had on our landscape.

However, the pattern of settlement within the Highlands has always been a transient

Ben Starav, Loch Etive.

one. In many areas the farming land is often only marginally arable, and historically it has proved very difficult for even relatively small populations to support themselves. Combined with other factors such as the notorious clearances of the nineteenth century, this resulted in a gradual emptying of the Highlands as people left arduous, poverty-stricken lives behind in search of a new start in the rapidly growing cities of Lowland Scotland or further afield in North America or Australia. The ruins that remain today are a poignant reminder of the struggle those people endured to survive in the Highlands. The legacy they have left behind is evident in the barren nature of the landscape that they once inhabited, denuded of its woodland and natural diversity. Ironically, though, it is the very emptiness which the escaping Highlanders left behind that now attracts so many visitors to the Scottish wilderness.

The story of human impact on the Highlands is by no means just a historical one. In more recent times road construction and the building of electricity pylons have left an unmistakable imprint on the landscape. One of the most controversial issues has been the advent of wind farms, with ever-increasing numbers of turbines becoming a dramatic example of contemporary interaction between humans and the landscape. Proponents of wind farms argue that they form an indispensable element of the drive towards renewable energy. Their detractors point out that the turbines have a massive impact on the landscape and that environmentalism should take aesthetic issues into account rather than concentrating entirely on carbon emissions; given the importance of tourism to the Highlands, the landscape, many argue, should not be sacrificed in the name of green energy.

The Highland landscape has become a key asset to the economy in many areas as walkers, climbers and photographers flock to the deserted glens, mountains and beaches. This is a particularly challenging environment for the photographer, as

The Skye Cuillin, Loch Scavaig.

Scotland's capricious weather can be every bit as dramatic as the social and geological history of the land it embraces. It is this ever-changing light that makes Scotland a virtual playground for the photographer.

A crucial element of landscape photography is being in the right place at the right time. This is far from being a matter of luck but instead the result of careful preparation. The vast majority of images in this book are premeditated, the end result of a process that begins with an idea or preconceived image. For each successful image a wide variety of factors must be taken into account: the position of the sun, the season, the time of day, wind, tides and weather all play significant roles.

Light is the essence of every image and fundamental to the art of photography; casting an infinite range of photographic possibilities upon the landscape, it is what makes every image unique. Capturing this light at its best as it interacts with the landscape is vitally important. The sun's position and the angle of light it projects upon the landscape are therefore a critical factor in the planning of a photograph. This is especially the case when photographing mountains, since particular features may only be in light for very limited periods of the day; images of north-facing aspects of mountains, where light can be an elusive and fleeting visitor, especially during the winter months, can be particularly difficult to capture. So for mountain photography knowledge of how the sun's position at a given time of the year will interact with the topography of the landscape, and when and where windows of light will open, is essential.

The seasons are a powerful force in our lives. They exist thanks to the fact that the Earth's axis is tilted at 23.5 degrees. As a result, different parts of the globe receive varying amounts of sunlight depending on their position in relation to the sun. Throughout the year as the Earth orbits the sun, this degree of exposure changes significantly. During the summer months, when the northern hemisphere is tilted towards the sun, the daylight will last longer and the sun's angle, or ecliptic, will

Moine House, Sutherland.

be higher in the sky. As the year progresses towards winter and the Earth continues its inexorable path around its star the northern hemisphere eventually finds itself tilted away from the sun, whose arc across the sky is lower, resulting in significantly shorter days. It is this process that this book will attempt to capture, charting the transformation of land and light as the seasons progress.

While the seasons transform the landscape over a period of months, the rotation of the Earth on its axis every twenty-four hours changes day into night. The period at the beginning and end of each day, as the sun rises or falls in the sky, is known to photographers as the 'golden hour'. This period is widely perceived as the ideal time of day to capture an image because of the quality of light. The spectacular red light cast by a dawn or sunset can render an otherwise mundane scene into something unique. Capturing this light in Scotland's wild places can be one of the most challenging aspects of photographing the Highland landscape. A shot taken at sunset from a mountain summit, for example, might require a descent in darkness; an image from the same location at dawn could require camping overnight on the mountain.

Scotland has an almost infinite range of possible compositions available to the more adventurous photographer who is prepared to leave the car behind and embrace the environment. It is no bad thing that some of Scotland's best-loved scenery is easily accessible to tourists and those less able make their way across the often difficult terrain of the Highlands. However, too many images seem to be taken from a handful of locations where the photographer barely needs to leave the side of the road. Missing out the well-known and over-exposed landmarks requires a little more imagination and commitment but can generate vastly more rewarding and distinctive results.

For example, to capture the photograph on page 102 of Loch Hourn I embarked on an undulating 5-mile/9-kilometre trek from Kinloch Hourn laden with camera and camping equipment. I captured the planned shot at 10.00 p.m. around the summer solstice, before spending a night camping, and made the long return journey the following day. Although this kind of trip can be hugely enjoyable it emphasizes the planning and preparation that is often required to turn the concept of an image into reality. The effort is always worthwhile because when a photograph long in planning and execution is captured, the results can be unforgettable.

However, even the best-laid plans are sometimes frustrated by the elements, which can act as friend or foe. A bank of cloud in the wrong place might obscure the fine light of dusk or dawn and ruin an image long in planning. At other times, however, a similar cloud may provide much-needed detail to an otherwise plain and featureless sky. Scotland's famously tempestuous weather is dominated by the combined effects of the warm North Atlantic Drift and the rain-bearing westerly air flow. Fuelled by the Atlantic this 'conveyor belt' drives continuous weather fronts towards Scotland, frequently leaving the mountain landscape shrouded in a seemingly impenetrable cloak of cloud and rain. The complex interaction between the weather fronts and Scotland's mountain ranges can make conditions very unpredictable. Having to operate in this unstable weather is part and parcel of landscape photography and a degree of experience, patience and luck is often required to capture any meaningful image.

Occasionally the volatility of the weather can work in the photographer's favour. The sunset image of a spectacular front developing over Loch Creran on page 110, for example, was the result of an abortive attempt to capture an image of Ben Cruachan across Loch Etive from the summit of Ben Sgulaird. Having set out in the early evening under clear skies I made good progress up the steep ridge towards the planned location for the shot. But on my arrival flat light and a featureless sky meant that the image of Ben Cruachan failed to live up to my expectations. Disappointed, I continued on to the summit and waited, in the hope that conditions would change. It was when I gave up and turned to the west to begin the long journey home that I witnessed the stunning sunset unfolding over Loch Creran. Thus, unlike most of my images, which are premeditated and planned quite meticulously, this photograph was the result of a chance encounter between the photographer, the volatile elements, the changing light and the landscape. In a sense, this encapsulates the experience of photographing in Scotland's weather: frustration can be replaced by inspiration in the time that it takes to turn around on a mountain ridge.

This, then, is the backdrop for landscape photography in Scotland: a land of great drama, be it geological or sociological or simply in terms of the boisterous weather that encompasses the magnificent landscape. The following portfolio of images, captured over six years, delves into the essence of this unique wilderness, the ever-changing seasons and the spectacular meeting of land and light. Ultimately, however, this captivating land will remain untamed, always capable of evoking new perceptions and fresh inspiration to all those who experience it.

Craig Aitchison

Rannoch Moor, Highland.

WINTER

Previous pages 16–17:

Loch Clair, Glen Torridon

Hasselblad XPan 45mm

February 2010

Standing on the shores of a frozen Loch Clair, I witnessed these natural colours of dawn flush the southern flanks of Liathach. As the moon set I was keen to make the image in this ethereal light before the sun rose.

Glen Coe, Highland

Hasselblad XPan 45mm

February 2007

Glen Coe is home to some of Scotland's most famous and notorious mountains. Captured at dawn from the summit of Beinn a' Chrulaiste, this image shows its southern aspect, which is made up of Buachaille Etive Mòr, Buachaille Etive Beag and the complex Bidean Massif, which contains a number of Munros alongside the Three Sisters and the well-known Lost Valley.

Sgùrr an Fhidhleir, Coigach

Hasselblad XPan 30mm

February 2011

Sgùrr an Fhidhleir rises like a shark's fin from the floor of the Coigach peninsula. This shapely summit is really a subsidiary peak of Ben More Coigach, where it forms the midway point in a magnificent rock buttress 3 miles/4.8 kilometres in length with cliffs that drop vertically 1,500 feet/457 metres down to the secluded Lochan Tuath.

Previous pages 20–21:

The Cuillin, Isle of Skye

Hasselblad XPan 45mm

January 2008

In winter the imposing coastal mountains of Skye take on a much more alpine appearance, reminiscent of the great European ranges of the Alps or Pyrenees. These precipitous peaks and ridges are mainly composed of basalt and the coarse-grained gabbro. This dark crystalline rock not only provides excellent grip for the thousands of walkers and climbers who visit each year but also gives the mountains the black from which the Black Cuillin derives its name.

The Isle of Rum, Inner Hebrides

Hasselblad XPan 45mm

January 2010

The Isle of Rum, once known as the Forbidden Isle, is actually the eroded vestiges of an ancient super-volcano that formed sixty million years ago. Relentless glaciations and constant weathering have produced one of the most distinctive mountain profiles on the western seaboard. The Rum Cuillin is a spectacular and intricate traverse composed of a number of summits, the highlight being the two Corbetts of Ainshval and Askival.

Glen Torridon, Wester Ross

Hasselblad XPan 30mm

February 2010

Glen Torridon is a classic example of a glaciated valley sculpted by the forces of nature. It is dominated by the giants of Liathach and Beinn Eighe, whose northern flanks rise steeply from the valley floor, forming a seemingly impenetrable wall of sandstone over 3,000 feet/914 metres high.

Previous pages 26–27:

Loch Coruisk, Isle of Skye

Hasselblad XPan 30mm

February 2010

Loch Coruisk lies deep in the heart of the Black Cuillin and is one of Scotland's truly wild places. It is almost completely enclosed on all sides and as a result is best viewed from the summit of Sgurr na Stri. At 1,630 feet/497 metres this remote peak is small in stature compared to its illustrious neighbours but it offers unsurpassed views of the loch and the entire Cuillin ridge. There are several adventurous routes to it. For my third attempt at this image I opted for the shorter but more strenuous 5-mile/9 kilometre trek from Kilmarie via Camasunary Bay.

Loch Lomond, Argyll and Bute

Hasselblad XPan 90mm

February 2008

For a relatively small hill the view on offer from
the summit of Duncryne is spectacular: a perfect
panorama of Loch Lomond and the surrounding
mountains of the southern Highlands. This
location is almost always best photographed
during winter at dawn, when the first rays of
sunlight illuminate the south-facing slopes.

The Black Mount, Rannoch Moor
Hasselblad XPan 45mm
February 2007

The perfectly formed profile of the Black
Mount range is often photographed from
the shores of Lochan na h-Achlaise. On this
occasion I wanted to climb a small unnamed
satellite peak that offered a different perspective
to this much celebrated Scottish landmark.

Previous pages 30–31 :
Ben Starav, Loch Etive
Hasselblad XPan 90mm
February 2008

Ben Starav lies at the head of Loch Etive and
dominates the skyline for miles around. This
majestic peak forms one side of a distinctively
glaciated U-shaped valley that is archetypal of
Scotland's western coastline.

Sgorr Dhearg, Highland
Hasselblad XPan 45mm
November 2010

I knew from experience that the view east
from the summit of Sgorr Dhearg offered
potential for good photography during the
winter months. After one failed attempt the year
before I took advantage of an early snowfall in
November and set off under perfect conditions.
On reaching the summit the winds were light
and the visibility superb with clear skies to the
west. I set up just below the summit and waited
for the right balance between light and shade,
before taking the shot.

Slioch, Lochan Fada

Hasselblad XPan 45mm

January 2011

With little wind to help disperse the blanket
of low-lying mist that had enveloped Lochan
Fada overnight, I had to wait for the sun to rise
sufficiently to burn it off. Eventually the scene
slowly revealed itself, but by that time the
east-facing slope of Slioch had slid into shadow.

Loch Tulla, Argyll and Bute
Hasselblad XPan 45mm
December 2010

The area around Loch Tulla supports an important remnant of the native Caledonian pine forest. Five thousand years ago these magnificent trees covered vast areas of Scotland's primeval wilderness. Today, however, thanks to millennia of overgrazing and ruthless deforestation only 1 per cent remains, all of it now heavily protected.

Garbh Beinn, Ardgour
Hasselblad XPan 90mm
December 2008

Garbh Beinn is seen by many from the main road that leads to Fort William. It rises majestically from the shores of Loch Linnhe to a height of 2,903 feet/885 metres, qualifying it for Corbett status. This image was made from the head of Loch Leven, where it appears to sit isolated from the mainland. Although it is part of the principal landmass it is seldom visited by climbers.

Castle Stalker, Loch Linnhe
Hasselblad XPan 90mm
December 2008

The peaks of the Morven peninsula provide
the perfect backdrop to this quintessential
Scottish scene. Situated on the shores of Loch
Linnhe, this castle has stood since 1320 and
changed ownership countless times. Today it
is privately owned and visits can even be made
by appointment. I made this photograph just
before a sunset in mid-winter when the last of
the afternoon light streams down the loch from
the west.

The Pap of Glencoe, Loch Leven

Hasselblad XPan 45mm

February 2007

Loch Leven is a typical example of the many
sea lochs found along the west coast of Scotland.
It stretches 9 miles/14 kilometres inland to the
small village of Kinlochleven and is surrounded
on all sides by steep, glaciated mountains. This
image shows Sgorr na Ciche, more commonly
known as the Pap of Glencoe. This distinctive
coastal peak is smaller in size compared to the
nearby Munros of Glencoe but lacks nothing
in character and profile.

Loch Maree, Wester Ross
Hasselblad XPan 90mm
February 2011

Loch Maree is one of Scotland's finest freshwater lochs. At its widest part it is peppered with around thirty wooded islands. Isolated and protected, these uninhabited havens are home to sea eagles, black-throated divers, wrens, otters and even red deer that are known to swim from the mainland. After two previously unsuccessful attempts I took advantage of a small but stable weather window when I made the short assent to my chosen location. I was keen to show these islands in relation to each other, with the dominating buttress of Slioch providing the perfect backdrop.

Loch Scavaig, Isle of Skye

Hasselblad XPan 45mm

December 2009

This classic view across Loch Scavaig toward the Black Cuillin requires little introduction. On this occasion I had to work quickly, as impending snow clouds, streaming down from the north, were threatening to block out the low afternoon sun. Fortunately I was able to make a number of images before the light disappeared for the rest of the day.

Previous pages 44–45:

Buachaille Etive Mòr, Glen Etive

Hasselblad XPan 45mm

February 2008

Buachaille Etive Mòr – the Great Herdsman of Etive – dominates the solitude of Rannoch Moor and the entrance to Glen Coe. It is one of Britain's most recognizable mountains and a favourite location for landscape photographers. After a long wait in changeable conditions a gap in the cloud finally opened and I managed to make a number of exposures before the light disappeared and the snow showers resumed.

Glamaig, Glen Sligachan
Hasselblad XPan 45mm
February 2008

From any angle the scree-covered slopes
of Glamaig could easily be mistaken for a
long-extinct volcano. At 2,543 feet/775 metres
this granite cone is one of only two Corbetts on
Skye and forms the northern end of the
Red Cuillin. Here a fleeting break in the
omnipresent cloudbank allowed me to capture
the last rays of light before the sun disappeared
over the horizon.

Loch Etive, Argyll and Bute

Hasselblad XPan 45mm

February 2009

Loch Etive stretches a total distance of 17 miles/27 kilometres inland from the open seas of the Firth of Lorn. It has to be one of Scotland's most beautiful lochs. The vast majority of its waters remain hidden from most because of the lack of road access into the area. For this photograph I positioned myself approximately halfway down the loch on the summit of a small hill. I waited for the sun to drop and clear a cloudbank, illuminating the landscape with warm evening light. The isolated farmhouse in the bottom right helps illustrate the vastness of this landscape.

The Cobbler, Argyll and Bute

Hasselblad XPan 45mm

December 2010

After some heavy snowfall during the winter of 2010
I made a late ascent of Ben Arthur, more commonly
known as the Cobbler. This iconic peak rises to 2,900
feet/884 metres from sea level and despite falling just
short of Munro status it is still a favourite among the
climbing community. The true summit takes the form
of an unusual rock formation, and negotiating this
tricky outcrop requires a head for heights and a crawl
through a natural opening in the rock affectionately
known as 'threading the needle'.

Moonen Bay, Isle of Skye
Hasselblad XPan 45mm
December 2009

The dramatic setting of Neist Point Lighthouse
marks the most westerly tip of the Isle of Skye.
Perched exposed on the Duirinish peninsula, it
has overlooked Moonen Bay since 1909. These
sheltered waters are one of the best places to
see whales, dolphins, basking sharks and the
numerous sea birds that nest in the cliffs of
Waterstein Head.

Fisherfield Forest, Wester Ross
Hasselblad XPan 30mm
January 2011

The view from the summit of Beinn Tarsuinn looks deep into the heart of the Fisherfield wilderness. This remote corner contains some of Scotland's best mountains, including An Teallach and the infamous Fisherfield six.

Lismore, Loch Linnhe

Hasselblad XPan 45mm

December 2010

The view east from Dùn da Ghaoithe on Mull is made up of many recognizable peaks, from Ben Cruachan on the right all the way to Ben Nevis on the left, some 37 miles/ 60 kilometres away. The serene nature of this image is contrary to the effort and logistics required to capture it. After boarding the early morning ferry from Oban to Craignure and walking 6 miles/10 kilometres to the intended location, I calculated I had only ten minutes to make a composition and exposure before starting the descent back in order to catch the last ferry to the mainland before Christmas!

The Black Cuillin, Isle of Skye

Hasselblad XPan 90mm

January 2008

The Black Cuillin is arguably the most dramatic of Scotland's mountain ranges. These jagged peaks and ridges account for eleven Munros and offer some of the most challenging mountaineering in the UK. Waiting patiently for the sun to rise, I witnessed the first rays of light strike the highest peaks, bathing them briefly in the pink light of dawn.

SPRING

Castlebay, Barra
Hasselblad XPan 90mm
April 2011

At 1,256 feet/383 metres, Sheabhal is the highest point on Barra, and unsurprisingly the summit gives wonderful Hebridean views in every quarter of the compass. With the Uists in the north, Skye and Rum to the west and the southern isles of Vatersay and the uninhabited Sandray, Pabbay and Mingulay. My original intention was to make the image without the inclusion of any passenger ferry, but by sheer chance I watched the early morning service depart for Oban and position itself perfectly.

Previous pages 58–59:
Ben Nevis, Loch Lochy
Hasselblad XPan 90mm
May 2008

Loch Lochy sits at the end of the Great Glen Fault which runs through Scotland from Inverness to Fort William. It is a freshwater loch which forms a major part of the Caledonian Canal network and also provides excellent views towards the towering Nevis Range of Lochaber.

Cùl Beag and Stac Pollaidh, Inverpolly

Hasselblad XPan 45mm

March 2009

The persistent haze of the day had forced me to rethink the shot I had originally intended on this particular evening. I decided to change my location and shoot directly into the sun, knowing that the haze would reduce the intensity of the sun and thus reduce the chances of lens flare. I firmly believe that part of being a successful photographer is having the ability to anticipate and adapt to changing conditions, especially in Scotland's notoriously unpredictable maritime climate.

South Uist, Outer Hebrides

Hasselblad XPan 45mm

May 2010

The entire west coast of South Uist is a
20–mile/32–kilometre continuous strip of
deserted virgin white sand. Backed by an
extensive dune system and the fertile machair
grasslands, this patchwork of habitats
is rich in plants and wildlife that are unique
to the Hebrides.

Glen Sligachan, Isle of Skye

Hasselblad XPan 45mm

May 2008

Glen Sligachan separates the rounded granite
peaks of the Red Cuillin (left) from the craggy
spires of the Black (right). The head of the glen
is dominated by the jagged profile of Sgurr
nan Gillean, one of Scotland finest and most
photogenic mountains.

Bidean nam Bian, Glen Coe

Hasselblad XPan 30mm

March 2009

In my opinion, some of Scotland's finest vistas are not from the highest summits but from lower, less recognized peaks. Meall Mor is one such. It is situated at the western end of Glen Coe, where it is frequently overshadowed by its more fashionable neighbours of the Aonach Eagach ridge and Bidean nam Bian. Consequently it can easily be disregarded as a worthwhile endeavour, but in fact the summit offers a grand and unique perspective into one of Scotland's most loved glens.

Loch Etive, Argyll and Bute
Hasselblad XPan 90mm
March 2009

I discovered this location by chance some
time ago when out exploring potential
viewpoints of Loch Etive. It was one of my
early photographic expeditions and at that
time I was shooting digitally, still learning
about the pitfalls of panoramic photography.
Disappointed with the results from my
previous attempts, I was keen to return to this
secluded corner and capture the image I had
found several years before.

Inverpolly, Sutherland

Hasselblad XPan 45mm

March 2007

The unmistakable mountains of the north-west Highlands are fashioned from the oldest strata found in Britain, some 3,000 million years old. Although not eminent in height, the individual profiles of Stac Pollaidh, Suilven, Cul Mòr, Cùl Beag and Beinn an Eoin have more character than most.

Loch Shiel, Sunart

Hasselblad XPan 45mm

March 2011

Stretching for 17 miles/27 kilometres inland to the head of Glenfinnan, Loch Shiel is the fourth-longest body of water in Scotland. The mountains enclosing this deep glaciated freshwater loch are extremely rough and seldom visited by climbers. This photograph was made at sunset from the northern flanks of Beinn Resipol, one of Scotland's finer Corbetts.

Stob Coire nan Lochan, Glen Coe
Hasselblad XPan 90mm
May 2007

The Bidean massif is the biggest mountain in
Glen Coe and the highest point in Argyll. The full
splendour of the mountain is only fully revealed
from above, where the conglomerate of corries,
ridges and peaks are laid out. It does not qualify for
Munro status but the giant north-east-facing cliffs
that make up Stob Coire nan Lochan are renowned
for having reliable rock climbing routes of all
grades throughout the seasons.

Coire an t-Sneachda, Cairn Gorm

Hasselblad XPan 45mm

March 2009

The natural mountain amphitheatre of Coire an t-Sneachda is home to some of the best and most accessible winter climbing in the UK. Its intricate snow-clad gulleys and chimneys have challenged technical climbers for generations. Also known as the Corrie of the Snows, this magnificent north-facing cirque is renowned for its vast accumulations of snow even long after winter has passed.

Previous pages 72–73:

Loch Tulla, Argyll and Bute

Hasselblad XPan 45mm

May 2007

Arriving early at the shores of Loch Tulla under typical spring-like conditions, I had hoped that a rainbow might appear at some point during the morning. Soon after I had set up, the mixture of sunshine and showers merged briefly to produce a perfectly placed low-arc rainbow exactly where I was looking. Surprised, I quickly took the photograph before the transient moment vanished.

Barra, Outer Hebrides

Hasselblad XPan 45mm

April 2011

Perched on the edge of Europe the Atlantic outpost of Barra is the most westerly inhabited island in Britain. For a relatively small island it has a remarkably diverse landscape, rich in photographic opportunities. The best of these are found on the west coast, where the deserted beaches are true Hebridean gems and the next stop west is Newfoundland, nearly 2,000 miles/3,218 kilometres away.

Montrose Bay, Angus
Hasselblad XPan 45mm
March 2008

Montrose Bay stretches for 5½ miles/8 kilometres
from the Montrose basin to the small village of St
Cyrus. This span of coast has a long association with
traditional salmon fishing, when stake nets were set
up on the low-lying sand to catch the precious fish as
they made their way from the sea to the mouth of the
River North Esk.

Top right:
Stac Pollaidh, Loch Lurgainn
Hasselblad XPan 45mm
March 2007

Stac Pollaidh is one of Scotland's most
recognizable peaks. Rising immediately
from the shores of Loch Lurgainn, it
has long been a favourite destination for
walkers and photographers alike. Access is
gained via a steep but well-maintained path
and the rewarding views of Assynt from
the summit rival that of any Munro.

Bottom Right:
Loch a' Gharbh-choire, Glenmore Forest
Hasselblad XPan 45mm
March 2009

Loch a' Gharbh-choire is an isolated lochan
situated high within the Rothiemurchus
Forest near Aviemore. It features some fine
examples of the protected Caledonian pine
tree that once covered vast areas of Scotland.

Glen Etive, Highland

Hasselblad XPan 30mm
March 2008

Beinn Trilleachan is a fine Corbett that overlooks
the head of Loch Etive, deep in Argyll. It is a
steep-sided peak that gives superb views of Glen
Etive, and the surrounding mountains. After a
steep ascent starting from sea level I reached
the summit with time to set up and appreciate
the scene that lay before me. I waited patiently
for the evening light to transform the landscape
in the way I had hoped for when I visualized
the image years before.

The Skye Cuillin, Isle of Raasay
Hasselblad XPan 45mm
April 2009

I had climbed to the summit of Dùn Caan, the highest point on the Isle of Raasay, the previous morning. Frustratingly I was presented with a persistent bank of low cloud refusing to break and obscuring the view towards the mountains of Skye that I had hoped to see. Twenty-four hours later, however, I was standing in exactly the same spot in the complete opposite of climatic conditions. The perfectionist in me had visualized something in between but with nature, more often than not you must take what you are given.

Black Mount, Rannoch Moor
Hasselblad XPan 45mm
May 2007

After an overnight camp I awoke to a marvellous sight: a sea of low-lying mist forming and streaming across the length of Rannoch Moor. The sun was rising into a thick veil of fog that cast a subtle light upon the landscape. Although this type of light is generally not suited to sweeping panoramas, I felt it added to the atmosphere of the morning and the moment.

Loch Druidibeag, South Uist

Hasselblad XPan 45mm

May 2010

The Loch Druidibeag Nature Reserve covers an
area of roughly 4,200 acres/1,700 hectares. This
relatively small area is home to a surprisingly
large variety of habitats, from a coastal marine
environment to moorland mountains. As a
result, this strong diversity is home to many
nationally important flowering plants, woodland
and wildlife. Because of this it is now recognized
as a Site of Special Scientific Interest and was
designated a UNESCO biosphere reserve in 1976.

Lochan Urr, Glen Etive

Hasselblad XPan 30mm

March 2007

This small but perfectly formed lochan is located three-quarters of the way down Glen Etive, sheltered on both sides by high-sided mountains. It is not uncommon to find striking reflections in it of the nearby mountains of Buachaille Etive Beag and Buachaille Etive Mòr.

Tràigh Mhòr, Barra

Hasselblad XPan 45mm

May 2010

The magnificent bay of Tràigh Mhòr lies at the north end of the Isle of Barra. This wide shallow beach with its hard, compact sand is used as the local airport and is the only runway in the world that is washed twice a day by the tide.

Previous pages 88–89:

The Three Sisters, Glen Coe

Hasselblad XPan 30mm

May 2009

The imposing triple buttress of Beinn Fhada, Gearr Aonach and Aonach Dudh, collectively known as the Three Sisters, forms a major part of Glen Coe's southern aspect. To show the full depth and majesty of these giant volcanic spurs, I wanted to gain as much altitude as possible. My third attempt to achieve this image coincided with an unseasonal cold spell that brought an overnight dusting of spring snow to the highest summits.

Loch Hourn, Knoydart
Hasselblad XPan 45mm
April 2010

Loch Hourn, arguably one of Scotland's most
beautiful sea lochs, lies within the undisturbed
wilderness of the Knoydart peninsula. Although
part of the mainland, it very often has the
atmosphere of some far-flung island, the sense
of isolation augmented by the lack of any roads.

Beinn a' Bheithir, Loch Leven

Hasselblad XPan 45mm

May 2007

Beinn a' Bheithir dramatically translates as
'Hill of the Thunderbolt'. Best viewed from the
northern shores of Loch Leven, this fabulously
sculpted mountain has the two principal Munro
summits of Sgorr Dhearg and Sgòrr Dhonuill,
which are normally climbed together via a
high-level ridge that forms a wonderful natural
horseshoe.

SUMMER

Carn Mór Dearg and Ben Nevis, Lochaber
Hasselblad XPan 30mm
June 2011

The north face of Ben Nevis is synonymous with extreme rock and ice climbing in Britain. In stark contrast to the rest of this famous mountain, the cliffs here drop vertically over 1,900 feet/600 metres deep into Coire Lies, offering a countless variety of routes all year round.

Previous pages 94–95:
Blà Bheinn, Isle of Skye
Hasselblad XPan 45mm
June 2007

Rising directly from sea-level, Blà Bheinn is thought to mean 'Blue Mountain' and is considered to be one of the finest mountains in Skye. I positioned myself on the shores of Loch Slapin and waited for the tide to recede sufficiently to expose the wonderfully sculpted rocks below.

Mullach an Rathain, Liathach

Hasselblad XPan 30mm

July 2011

The heavily glaciated Torridonian giants of Ben Alligin, Beinn Eighe and Liathach are considered to be some of the finest mountains in Britain. These seemingly impenetrable sandstone 'castles' sit in proud isolation, rising steeply from an ancient bedrock of Lewisian gneiss that dates back to around 3,000 million years ago. This photograph shows the view north from Mullach an Rathain, the western summit of Liathach that overlooks Beinn Eighe and the Flowerdale Forest.

Loch Hourn, Barrisdale Bay

Konica Minolta 5D 18–70mm

June 2006

Barrisdale Bay lies in the heart of the Knoydart peninsula on the shores of Loch Hourn. Relatively isolated, it is accessed via a well-maintained stalker's path that follows the undulating contours of Loch Hourn's steep-sided south shore. After an enjoyable walk in I pitched my tent and waited for the sun to set over the loch. A persistent haze had been gradually building up throughout the day and this helped to naturally filter and intensify the evening light, making a spectacular sunset.

Previous pages 100–101:

The Isle of Harris, Outer Hebrides

Hasselblad XPan 45mm

August 2007

The west coast of Harris is famous for its unspoilt sandy beaches and rocky coast. Exposed to the full wrath of the Atlantic weather, this environment is constantly changing. As always it was a thrill to be working in such unpredictable conditions and I recall having to wait until the very end of day for the light to finally clear the remnants of another passing squall.

Ben Starav, Rubha Bharr

Hasselblad XPan 45mm

June 2010

This secluded bay lies at the end of a fine forestry track that runs along the north shore of Loch Etive. The deciduous woodland in this area has been designated a Special Area of Conservation because of the diverse mixture of mature Caledonian pine, oak, elm, hazel and yew trees that thrive in this natural isolated nursery.

Am Buachaille, Sandwood Bay

Hasselblad XPan 45 mm

July 2007

The prominent and picturesque sandstone sea stack of Am Buachaille lies at the south-western tip of Sandwood Bay. First climbed in 1967, it stands 215 feet/65 metres high, defiant against the relentless elements, just south of Cape Wrath on the Sutherland coast.

Coigach, Inverpolly
Hasselblad XPan 30mm
June 2009

Cul Mòr stands in the middle of
Inverpolly and commands one of the best
summit viewpoints in the north-west
Highlands. After a number of previous
trips I knew that the optimum time to
make this photograph would be as close to
the summer solstice as possible. Timing
this image accordingly, I was fortunate to
find perfect conditions and captured Cùl
Beag, Stac Pollaidh and the mountains
of Coigach as the sun set at its most
northerly.

Sanna Bay, Ardnamurchan

Hasselblad XPan 90mm

July 2007

Perched on the very western tip of the British mainland, Sanna Bay is perfectly positioned to enjoy some fine views of Skye and the Small Isles. The jewel in the crown, however, is the magnificent stretch of pristine white sand and the crystal-clear turquoise waters for which Scotland's north-western coast is renowned.

Oldshoremore, Sutherland
Hasselblad XPan 30mm
August 2010

Oldshoremore beach sits nestled among high
sand dunes in the barren landscape of Scotland's
far north-west. Despite it being voted one of
Britain's best beaches, Oldshoremore's isolated
location means that it is not uncommon to have
this sweeping expanse of unspoilt beach all
to yourself.

Previous pages 108–109
Loch Creran, Appin
Hasselblad XPan 30mm
June 2010

I had climbed Ben Sgulaird with the full
intention of photographing Ben Cruachan
across Loch Etive. However, upon arriving,
the scene and weather conditions failed to meet
my expectations. With the opportunity to make
a worthwhile photograph now diminished
I turned around and retraced my steps. I was
still high up when a beautiful sunset started to
develop as the tail of a retreating weather front
was spectacularly lit up by the setting sun as it
dipped below the mountains of Mull and the
Kingairloch peninsula.

Loch Shiel, Sunart
Hasselblad XPan 30mm
August 2010

In 2010 an unseasonal dry spell during July
and August left many of the freshwater lochs
in Scotland at an all-time low. With local rivers and
streams reduced to nothing more than a trickle,
the water of Loch Shiel slowly drained away to
reveal a temporary new landscape of rocks and
sand that are normally hidden from view.

Ben Starav, Glen Etive

Hasselblad XPan 45mm

June 2009

Like a fossilized sleeping dragon, Ben Starav is
the dominant hill of the Etive peaks. It rises
steeply from the enclosed confines of Glen
Etive and is therefore particularly difficult to
photograph. Having climbed a smaller summit on
the opposite side of the glen, I set about exploring
potential viewpoints that would show the true
grandeur of one of my favourite mountains.

Ben Cruachan, Argyll and Bute
Hasselblad XPan 30mm
June 2010

This magnificent mountain is one of the giants
of the southern Highlands. Its soaring ridges
and satellite peaks culminate in the two Munro
summits of Ben Cruachan and Stob Diamh.
These are linked by an exposed high-level ridge
that rarely drops below the 2,952-foot/
900-metre mark.

Gruinard Bay, Wester Ross

Hasselblad XPan 30mm

June 2009

Gruinard Bay is nestled within the rocky coastline of Wester Ross. Its distinctive pinkish sand originates from the Torridonian sandstone that surrounds it. This location is very easily accessed and while waiting for low tide I watched from my elevated position as two slow-moving basking sharks skirted the headland and entered the bay.

Cir Mhor, Isle of Arran

Hasselblad XPan 45mm

July 2011

After an overnight camp and an early start,
I reached the summit of Caisteal Abhail with
just enough time to set my camera up and catch
the first rays of early morning light striking the
backbone of the Arran mountains and beyond
to Ailsa Craig.

Old Man of Storr, Isle of Skye

Hasselblad XPan 45mm

June 2007

The Old Man of Storr stands dominant overlooking the Sound of Raasay on Skye's east coast. This remarkable piece of rock architecture is the result of numerous landslides thought to have occurred approximately 6,500 years ago. On this morning, thanks to the exceptional air clarity, I was able to discern many recognizable peaks, from Ben Nevis in the south all the way north to the unmistakable mountains of Coigach and beyond – a total distance of over 75 miles/120 kilometres.

Barra, Outer Hebrides

Hasselblad XPan

August 2009

After a typical Hebridean day of sunshine and showers, I watched as another rain squall swept in from the Atlantic. Stranded in the deluge, I stayed and gradually the ancient landscape was revealed in the warm evening light. Out to the west the skies remained clear and I was able to photograph the rugged coast as the tail end of the weather front finally cleared and disappeared to the east.

Loch Sunart, Lochaber

Hasselblad XPan 30mm

August 2010

Ben Hiant forms the highest point on the Ardnamurchan peninsula. At only 1,730 feet/ 528 metres high it is a small mountain but it commands stunning views across the head of Loch Sunart and south towards the Sound of Mull. The sailing boat centre right illustrates the scale while Ben More, Mull's only Munro, is dominant to the west.

Sandwood Bay, Sutherland

Hasselblad XPan 45mm

July 2007

Sandwood Bay is one of the most beautiful and isolated beaches in the British Isles. Lying at the end of a 4-mile/6.5-kilometre track, this magnificent stretch of coastline has everything: sea cliffs, sand dunes and the landmark sea stack of Am Buachaille.

The Small Isles, Inner Hebrides

Hasselblad XPan 45mm

August 2008

From an elevated position above the small village of Arisaig I witnessed the remnants of a weather front finally dissipating and breaking up in the late evening light. The blustery westerly wind had also subsided and I was able to make the photograph as the sun set over the Small Isles of Muck, Eigg and Rum.

Assynt, Highland

Hasselblad XPan 45mm

August 2011

This remarkable ancient landscape is one of Scotland's best and it can offer fine photographic opportunities to those who are willing to explore it. This photograph was made from the summit of Beinn an Eoin, a mountain often overlooked by walkers and one with no obvious path. After negotiating my way to the top I stood on the windless summit amidst a cloud of midges as a large front of threatening cloud moved in from the south. Fortunately the sky to the north remained clear and I was able to shoot the image I had hoped for before the light was snuffed out by the rapidly advancing cloud bank.

Loch Lomond, Argyll and Bute

Hasselblad XPan 45mm

July 2009

Shot from the quieter, less frequented east
shore of Loch Lomond, this image shows
the profusion of greens that envelope
the land during June, July and August.
Fortunately this overbearing colour was
appeased by the waters of the loch reflecting
a wonderful summer sky above.

Sgorr Dhearg, Beinn a Bheithir
Hasselblad XPan 45mm
August 2007

After a steep ascent from sea level I positioned myself just below the summit of Sgorr Dhonuill with the aim of photographing the neighbouring peak of Sgorr Dhearg. Standing high above the vast corrie of Gleann a' Chaolais, I was able to see clearly the great whaleback of Ben Nevis, with the compact Mamores group providing the perfect background in the evening light.

AUTUMN

Loch Quoich, Lochaber
Hasselblad XPan 30mm
November 2008

Loch Quoich stretches 8 miles/13.5 kilometres, straight into the heart of the rough bounds of Knoydart. Because of the huge natural rainfall catchment in this area the loch was dammed in 1956 and used as the main storage reservoir for the Garry Hydro Scheme. The waters were forced upwards of over 100 feet/30 metres, displacing a number of settlements and creating a completely new shoreline within this land of mountain and flood.

Previous pages 132–133:
Inverpolly, Sutherland
Hasselblad XPan 45mm
September 2010

Overlooking Achnahaird Bay, Cnoc Mòr is well positioned for uninterrupted views of the Inverpolly mountains. I had long thought that this tiny hillock would make an excellent vantage point if the conditions were right. Fortunately I timed my arrival perfectly and witnessed the remnants of a ferocious weather system as it finally cleared the mountains of Cul Mòr, Stac Pollaidh, Beinn an Eoin and Ben more Coigach.

Abhainn Shira, Bridge of Orchy

Hasselblad XPan 45mm

November 2009

Collectively known as the Great Wall of Rannoch, Beinn Achaladair, Beinn an Dòthaidh and Beinn Dorain act as a gateway to the wilderness of Rannoch Moor and beyond to Glen Coe. On a perfect winter's afternoon, I made my way along the banks of Abhainn Shira, searching for a position I had identified months before. I set my camera and tripod up on the banks and waited for the sun to drop. As the warm evening light began to flood the landscape I used a slow shutter speed to soften the torrent of water as it flowed past my feet.

Torrisdale Bay, Bettyhill
Hasselblad XPan 30mm
October 2010

Torrisdale Bay is situated on the north coast of
Scotland, close to the tiny village of Bettyhill.
This beautiful sweep of sand runs for over
1 mile/0.8 kilometres and is backed by an
extensive dune system and salt marsh. It is also
a popular surfing spot and on this particular
morning the huge waves crashing ashore were
indicative of the tremendous wind speed, which
made conditions for photography marginal at
best. Fortunately I was able to find a degree of
shelter behind a drystone dyke, which allowed
me to photograph the windswept bay and
turbulent sky above.

Previous pages 138–139:
Loch Etive, Argyll and Bute
Hasselblad XPan 45mm
September 2010

On a perfect early autumn morning I found
myself on the shores of Loch Etive. After a
6–mile/10.5-kilometre cycle from Inverawe
I arrived at Rubha Àird Rainich to a place of
absolute stillness. Surrounded by the mountains
of Lorn and these pristine conditions, I felt it
a privilege to be alone in such an environment.
Aware that such moments are rare, I
immediately set my camera up to capture the
extraordinary scene. This was the very first
frame I took, and minutes later the wind picked
up and the reflection vanished.

The Isle of Skye, Kyle of Lochalsh
Hasselblad XPan 45mm
September 2008

This image of the Skye Cuillin at sunset illustrates the fact that although the vast majority of my photographs are planned in advance, sometimes unexpected opportunities present themselves. On a return journey from Harris, while crossing the Skye bridge I could see the cloud fragment and the light begin to change. I frantically headed for some high ground in the hope of catching the rapidly unfolding scene. Fortunately I found a position with literally seconds to spare and was able quickly to shoot a small number of frames before the sun fell below the horizon.

Loch Lomond, Argyll and Bute
Hasselblad XPan 90mm
October 2008

Loch Lomond is one of Scotland's
most famous bodies of water. Despite
its obvious natural beauty I still find it
incredibly difficult to photograph. After
several failed attempts I finally found
this position in some farmland, midway
along the south shore. From here I could
see the scale of the loch, its islands and
the mountains that make this area one of
Britain's most visited national parks.

Loch Cul Dromannan, Coigach

Hasselblad XPan 45mm

October 2008

This small sheltered lochan lies close to the main road that cuts through this extraordinary landscape. Thanks to its position, it provides an easily accessible 'window' on to Stac Pollaidh and the mountains of Coigach. I had made a number of visits to this popular spot over the years and finally succeeded in capturing the perfect reflection I was seeking.

Loch Tulla, Argyll and Bute

Hasselblad XPan 45mm

November 2010

The fresh water of Loch Tulla sits close to the tiny hamlet of Bridge of Orchy in the Central Highlands. Surrounded by high mountains and remnants of the ancient Caledonian pinewoods, this is an area of countless photographic opportunities.

Ardmaddy Bay, Loch Etive
Hasselblad XPan 45mm
October 2009

Many photographers have their favourite locations to
which they return time after time and mine is Loch
Etive, particularly the area surrounding Ardmaddy Bay.
Reaching this location requires a long walk, although
the journey can be considerably eased by the use of a
mountain bike. I had visited this area every month of the
year and eventually decided that a low tide on an autumn
morning would allow me to capture this beautiful corner
of Scotland at its best.

The Birks of Aberfeldy, Perthshire
Konica Minolta 5D 18–70mm
October 2005

After a night of particularly heavy rain,
the swollen waters of the Moness Burn cut
relentlessly through the steeply wooded glen
known as the Birks of Aberfeldy. At the very
end of October, when the autumn colours are at
their height, I found a flat section of this famous
river and waited for the sun to light the canopy
of golden foliage above.

Duncryne Hill, Loch Lomond

Hasselblad XPan 45mm

November 2009

The islands of Loch Lomond form part of
the Highland Boundary Fault line, which
stretches across Scotland from Arran to
Stonehaven and separates the Highlands
and Lowlands. The beauty and tranquillity
of the loch that we see here belie by the
tremendous geological upheaval that
created the fault.

Loch Katrine, Stirlingshire

Hasselblad XPan 30mm

October 2010

Having arrived at the summit of Ben A'an well before dawn, I watched the early morning mist ebb and flow down the length of the loch. As the sun rose into a milky sky, I was eager to make the photograph with this wonderful addition before it dissipated into the cold October air.

Slioch, Loch Maree

Hasselblad XPan 30mm

October 2008

The imposing tower buttress of Slioch is arguably one of Scotland's most photogenic mountains. It dominates the shore of Loch Maree, where it sits isolated and apparently almost impenetrable from all sides. Fortunately access is relatively easy, by means of a well-trodden path that cuts through a vast and hidden corrie on the east side of this iconic mountain.

Oldshoremore, Sutherland

Hasselblad XPan 45mm

October 2009

Natural displays of intense light such as this happen rarely
in Scotland, usually when least expected. The day had been
particularly wet, with persistent low cloud covering the
mountain tops since dawn. With the forecast predicting that
the stubborn front would clear I decided to head for the coast.
I arrived an hour before sunset to see a thin strip of clear sky
just above the horizon. As the evening developed, the sun
passed though the opening, transforming the grey cloud into a
wondrous display of colour.

Ben Loyal, Sutherland
Hasselblad XPan 45mm
October 2009

Ben Loyal – Queen of the Scottish mountains
– is one of the most northerly Corbetts in
Scotland. Rising to 2,507 feet/764 metres and
overlooking the Kyle of Tongue, this granite
peak soars majestically from a vast expanse of
open moorland. Its instantly recognizable profile
is due to its craggy top, which contains four
major peaks, the highest of which is An Caisteal.

Loch Eil, Lochaber
Hasselblad XPan 45mm
September 2009

As I sat on the silent shores of Loch Eil waiting for some cloud to form, my attention was grabbed from behind by the sound of splashing water. I turned around slowly to observe an otter feeding on small crabs among the kelp. This wonderful sight was sufficiently far away that I did not disturb the otter. And fortunately for me the otter's movements did not upset the perfectly still water reflecting the rugged mountains of Glenfinnan.

Loch Achray, Stirlingshire

Hasselblad XPan 45mm

October 2009

The Trossachs are renowned as being one of the best areas in the country to see the spectacular onset of autumn. This compact wooded area contains an exceptionally diverse array of deciduous trees, ensuring that each year there is an unparalleled blaze of colour on display through October and into November. The area is also peppered with a number of lochs. Loch Achray is one of the smallest, and its placid waters make it an ideal location for exquisite reflections of Ben Venue and the surrounding woodland.

Caledonian Pine, Victoria Bridge
Hasselblad XPan 90mm
November 2009

This image epitomizes much that is best about the Scottish Highlands. The magnificent solitary Caledonian pine is emblematic of the sweeping woodland that once dominated the landscape. I had been planning this composition for some time and was fortunate to find a pair of stags silhouetted on the horizon as the sun set in the west.

The Kyle of Tongue, Sutherland
Hasselblad XPan 30mm
October 2009

The north coast of Scotland is awash with
steep cliffs, sheltered bays and long shallow
inlets. One of the largest of these estuaries
is the sweeping Kyle of Tongue, where the
intertidal sandbanks and mud flats extend a
whole 6 miles/10 kilometres inland. I spent
a wonderful afternoon exploring this area
and stumbled across this striking prospect.
The cloud had been building during the day
and I composed the shot more in hope than
expectation. I was about to give up when
suddenly the sun broke through for long
enough to transform the scene.

Inverpolly, Sutherland

Hasselblad XPan 90mm

October 2009

Under a stormy October sky I ventured up the tiny mound of Meall an Fheadain situated near Achiltibuie. Although it is only 600 feet/ 183 metres high, the wind speed at the summit was severely hindering any attempt at photography and I was forced to retreat and seek shelter behind a conveniently placed radio mast. Safe from the buffeting wind, I waited for a break in the cloud and watched the fleeting light strike the unmistakable skyline of the Inverpolly mountains.

Loch Awe, Inchnadamph
Hasselblad XPan 30mm
October 2008

A week spent in Ullapool amidst typically
tempestuous autumnal weather had left me
unable to capture any of my planned images.
But the elements finally relented and my
patience was rewarded as the calm following
the storm provided the conditions I had been
waiting for. The heavy snowfall on Canisp
was in stark contrast to the rich colours that
prevailed at lower level along the shore of
Loch Awe.

Ben Cruachan, Argyll and Bute

Hasselblad XPan 45mm

October 2010

The onset of autumn prompts a dramatic change across the landscape. The monotonous blanket of green that can choke the environment is gradually replaced by autumn's rich colour palette. To the photographer this natural injection of colour provides the much-needed contrast that can be so difficult to find during the summer months. This image was shot from the north shore of Loch Etive, looking south towards the imposing crags and corries of Ben Cruachan as they were thrown into sharp relief by the setting sun.

CHASING THE LIGHT

BARRA

The small island of Barra is home to some of the wildest and most beautiful locations in the UK. It lies at the south-west of the Outer Hebrides and its west coast, exposed to the full force of the Atlantic, has a number of spectacular, unspoilt sandy beaches. Although it is well to the west of the Scottish mainland, Barra is easily accessible by both air and sea.

I caught the ferry from South Uist in the mid-morning, planning to capture an image of Tràigh Mhòr and Tràigh Eais from the summit of Beinn Eireabhal. After the short ferry trip across the Sound of Barra, I set off on my mountain bike for the thirty-minute ride to the base of the hill. Although relatively short in stature at 650 feet/198 metres, Beinn Eireabhal commands stunning panoramic views of Barra itself and north towards South Uist. At the summit, despite the beautiful blue sky the strong westerly wind made photography impossible and I was forced to head lower down to seek a more sheltered location. Fortunately I was still able to compose the desired shot of the magnificent landscape laid out before me.

Although it is not obvious at first glance, Tràigh Mhòr has served for many years as the island's airport: flights arrive and depart regularly at low tide and it is now the only beach airport in the world to be used for scheduled airline services. A narrow strip of land separates this from Tràigh Eais, a truly stunning expanse of sandy beach that runs for almost 1½ miles/2.5 kilometres along the island's west coast. An Atlantic gale can result in spectacular surf conditions along this beach, although the water temperature may deter all but the hardiest of surfers.

BEN NEVIS

The highest mountain in the British Isles, Ben Nevis is also one of the most dramatic. A mountain of great contrasts, it can appear relatively benign from some angles and can be easily climbed via the tourist track that snakes its way up the western flank of the mountain. However, the legions of walkers who plod up the tourist track each year miss the extraordinary drama of the mountain's north face – an experience that Cameron McNeish, one of Scotland's foremost climbers and journalists, has described as 'going to the beach and never seeing the sea'.

A far more interesting and rewarding visit to Ben Nevis can be had by traversing around the north of the mountain and ascending Carn Mòr Dearg, from where the Carn Mòr Dearg arête leads to the summit of Ben Nevis itself. This route has the vast benefit of exposing the mountain's huge and intimidating north face, complete with cliffs of over 2,000 feet/610 metres and some of the most difficult and historic climbing routes in Britain.

For this image, my plan was to ascend the tourist track as far as the halfway lochan (Lochan Meall an t-Suidhe, to give it its proper name), but then head around the north face and ascend towards Carn Mòr Dearg, setting up somewhere on the ridgeline between Carn Mòr Meadhonach and Carn Mòr Dearg. I reached position in fine weather with the north face in ideal light. There was an unusual, almost eerie, stillness in the air as I set up the camera. The strong winds that normally prevail over ridges at this altitude were absent, and the total silence was as dramatic as the scene that lay before me.

THE ISLE OF EIGG

The Small Isles – Rum, Eigg, Canna and Muck – sit relatively close to Scotland's west coast and together form a major part of the Inner Hebrides archipelago. Eigg, the second largest, is a favourite destination for the adventurous photographer. Its seclusion and unique geological features always make the eighty-minute crossing from Mallaig worthwhile. The jewel in its crown is hidden on its north-west coast: the pristine and unspoilt Bay of Laig. It is perhaps most visited in summer, for the beauty of the renowned Singing Sands with their unsurpassed view towards the ominous Rum Cuillin. I had felt for a long time that this classic view would be at its best during the winter months, when low light and a dusting of snow would add a sense of drama and depth to an image.

Given the remote nature of the location and the short winter days, this shot required a well-planned expedition. An opportunity arose in January 2010 and I departed early for Mallaig to catch the ferry. That morning the stars were out, the sky was clear and as my car's headlights cut through the twilight of Rannoch Moor the temperature on my dashboard read –17°C.

As the ship headed south-west out of Mallaig harbour, stunning panoramic views began to unfold: the distinctive outline of Eigg ahead, the Rum Cuillin to the west and to the north the magnificent, mountainous profile of Skye. This unique vista makes the ferry journey a very enjoyable outing in itself at any time, but on this day an unforgettable bonus lay in wait, as a pod of dolphins joined the ferry, effortlessly riding its bow wave as we headed across the Sound of Sleat.

I would have one hour and forty-five minutes on the island before the ferry was due to return to the mainland; it was not to return to the island again for several days. Laig Bay lies 4 miles/6.5 kilometres north-west from where the ferry lands, at the end of the island's only road. A brisk half-hour cycle along the icy road got me into position and I was relieved to find perfect conditions for the shot. Forty-five minutes passed while I set up the camera, captured some images and packed up again. The return cycle journey was an interesting one, as I could see the ferry approaching. Fortunately I made it on time, with just minutes to spare.

FISHERFIELD

A shot of the Fisherfield mountains entails a trip to one of the most remote and beautiful areas of the Highlands. A long drive took me to Kinlochewe, where I left the car and embarked on a mountain bike ride into the wilderness. A Land Rover track follows a stream into the mountains. A bridge crosses the stream before the track narrows into a path, which eventually fades away altogether. Here, I abandoned the bike and proceeded on foot.

A steep 4-mile/6.5-kilometre walk lay before me, towards Lochan Fada and the summit of Beinn Tarsuinn. A golden eagle was in the sky above, as always a breathtaking sight. As I continued upwards, one bird of prey was replaced by another as an RAF Tornado thundered past. Military jets are a common sight in the Highlands, but I later discovered that this one met an unhappy fate just minutes after I had seen it, crashing into Loch Ewe. Fortunately its crew escaped unscathed.

I reached the summit and set up the camera, awestruck by the majestic view before me. An Teallach, that most iconic of Scotland's mountains, lay to the north, with three of Fisherfield's six Munros linked by a ridge in the foreground to the east. The panorama was completed by Slioch to the south-west and Scotland's most remote Munro, A'Mhaighdean, to the west. The shot that I had planned effectively framed An Teallach between the ridge to the east and Beinn Dearg Mòr to the west. Conditions were ideal for photography and, having captured the image, it was with some regret that I left the stunning viewpoint behind and began the long journey back to the car.

This was not without incident, as I discovered, much too late, that the aforementioned bridge was covered in black ice. My mountain bike careered over the side of the bridge and plummeted into the gorge below – fortunately without its rider, who lay in a rather embarrassed heap just short of the edge. With a damaged bike, and injured pride, I walked back to the car.

INVERPOLLY

It is often said that the most interesting and dynamic light can be found at the edge of weather fronts as bad weather departs and is replaced by better conditions, and so it was to prove as I headed towards Sutherland for a long-planned shot of the Sgùrr an Fhidhleir. I found myself driving through some of the worst weather I have ever seen in Scotland, with torrential rain making driving conditions hazardous and photography the last thing on my mind.

Upon reaching Ullapool, however, the conditions began to improve. The band of weather receded south-eastwards and the sky began to brighten. With my shot of the Sgùrr an Fhidhleir not planned until the following day, I sensed an opportunity to capture a shot of the landscape embraced by the volatile conditions and drove another forty-five minutes north to Coigach.

Previous experience of this area led me to a slightly elevated position looking over Achnahaird Bay and south-east towards the mountains of Inverpolly and Coigach. The sky was changing minute by minute, the weather front seeming to drag an all-encompassing sheet behind it, leaving a clear sky to the west and beautiful, dynamic cloud formations to the east. This shot demonstrates that while the majority of landscape photography is premeditated it can pay to be flexible and take advantage of the drama created by changing conditions.

KNOYDART

Knoydart is one of the UK's most rewarding environments for landscape photography, but among the most challenging. A genuine wilderness, it is home to some of the country's finest mountains, which tower over Loch Hourn. Stunning panoramas abound, with views out to the Isle of Skye and the Outer Hebrides beyond. My objective, however, was to capture an image looking inland from the north-eastern flanks of Ladhar Beinn. This perspective of Loch Hourn beautifully encapsulates the fjord-like nature of many Scottish sea lochs, cut into the landscape by retreating glaciers and framed by surrounding mountains.

The closest road ends in Kinloch Hourn, about 10 miles/16 kilometres from the location I had in mind. Walking to Ladhar Beinn from here requires a long undulating walk and at least one night's camping. It is also possible to approach from the south of the peninsula by catching the ferry from Mallaig to Inverie. This requires an equally daunting walk over the Màm Barrisdale pass. Past experience has shown me that such walks can be immensely rewarding but on this occasion I chose a third option: driving to Arnisdale and catching the ferry across Loch Hourn from the north.

The 'ferry' consists of a small boat with an outboard motor, which goes to various locations around the loch. The crossing is speedy but noisy, and is a marvellous experience, with a view of the loch and its surrounding mountains that is never less than inspiring. The boat deposited me at the bay at Poll à Mhuineil. As I watched it continue on its way I was immediately struck by the silence, and the sense of absolute wilderness that prevails in Knoydart.

I headed for my chosen location at around 1,000 feet/305 metres on Ladhar Beinn. This provided the elevation necessary to capture the head of the loch far inland while maintaining an interesting foreground. After a short wait the light conditions were ideal and I captured the image. Returning to meet the boat I was mindful not to be late: Knoydart is not somewhere to spend an unscheduled night in the wild! But working in this incredible environment, alone with my camera, is a privilege, and an experience that makes all the problems of access seem trivial indeed.

LOCH CORUISK

One of the jewels in the crown of the Scottish Highlands is undoubtedly Skye's majestic Cuillin ridge. Nestled in the midst of this magnificent vista is Loch Coruisk, seen here from the summit of Sgurr na Stri. All eleven Munros of the Cuillin ridge are visible from this vantage point, surely one of the finest viewpoints in Britain.

Having left my car at Kilmarie, I began the long and undulating walk towards the bay of Camasunary. Looking towards Bla Bheinn I paused to watch a pair of sea eagles soaring high above the mountain's ridges, a stunning sight epitomizing all that is best about the Scottish wilderness. Once across Camasunary it is necessary to ford a river; with the waters swollen by the November rain this was a slightly daunting prospect. With this obstacle negotiated I walked along the eastern flank of Sgurr na Stri before ascending from the north.

As I approached the summit, the silence was broken by a dramatic beating of wings as another eagle departed from the mountain top. I was much closer this time and stood mesmerized by the sight of the magnificent bird of prey, silhouetted in the morning sun, as it glided into the distance. I wondered if this was one of birds I had seen over Bla Bheinn and envied its ability to cover the landscape with such effortless speed and grace.

Turning to the west I began to compose my shot of the Cuillin ridge. Compared to its neighbouring Munros, Sgurr na Stri has a relatively lowly peak at just over 1,600 feet/488 metres, but it is sufficiently high and exposed to command an unbroken view over the ridge with Loch Coruisk in the foreground.

SANDWOOD BAY

Arguably the most magnificent beach in the British Isles, Sandwood Bay lies on the north-western tip of Sutherland just south of Cape Wrath. The closest point of access by road is Blairmore, roughly a 4-mile/6.5-kilometre walk from the bay. Apart from the sense of splendid isolation as one walks through one of the least populated regions anywhere in Western Europe, the walk to the beach has little to recommend it and gives scant indication of the delights that await upon reaching the coast. The noise of the Atlantic rollers crashing ashore is the first warning of the beach ahead before the glorious sight of the 1-mile/2.5-kilometre stretch of pristine sand unfolds. Despite its unrivalled beauty, Sandwood Bay is remote enough to deter the casual sightseer, which means that it is not unusual to find oneself alone on the beach. This solitude and the full force of the Atlantic weather systems marching ashore give you a thrilling sense of being in the wild.

Photography in this part of the country often falls victim to the volatile weather, and so it proved when I visited the bay to find strong winds and driving rain precluding any possibility of capturing a meaningful image. The trip was not wasted, however, as I was able to spend some time studying the bay and finding the ideal location for a shot that really encapsulated its scale and majesty. The following day I returned to find much-improved weather and headed for the chosen location on elevated ground at the south-western end of the beach, close to Am Buachaille, Sandwood's iconic sea stack.

Although the skies had cleared, a strong northerly wind was hitting the foot of the cliff and the air was being forced upwards towards my position. This meant that even when using a tripod I had to be very careful to avoid camera shake. Sandwood's scale and grandeur are epitomized by the fact that in the shot the seemingly deserted beach is in fact occupied by one person (my wife), who is scarcely visible, standing beside the rocky outcrop centre right of picture.

INDEX

MAP

Numbers indicate the location at which the photographs were taken
and the page numbers in which they appear

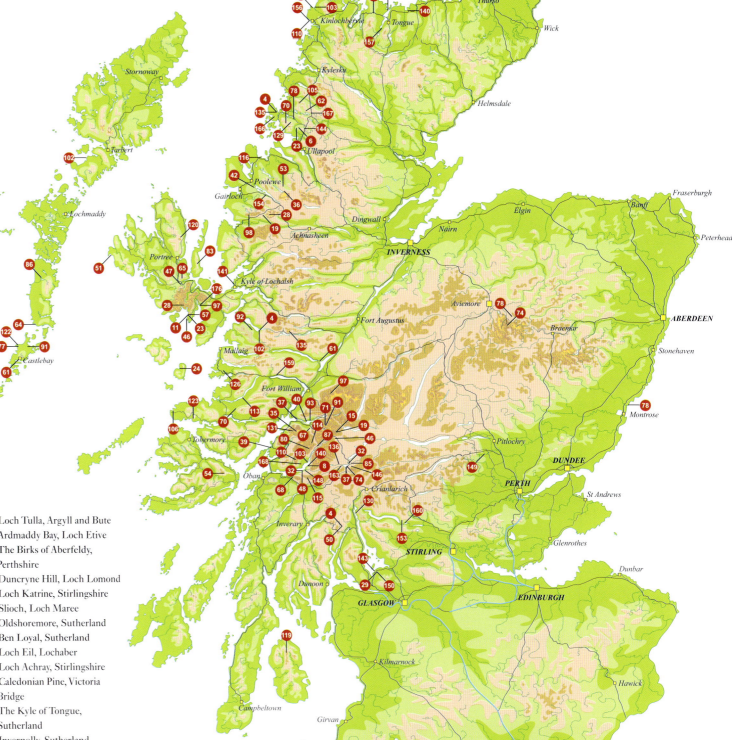

175

ABOUT THE PHOTOGRAPHY

My exposure to Scotland's mountain areas began at a young age with family holidays to Fort William, Aviemore and Skye. I can remember being dragged up Stob Coire Nan Lochan at twelve years old by my father, ice axe in hand and not quite appreciating the environment I was in. Even back then I was using a camera, but mostly taking pictures of trains on the West Highland line.

My interest in photography developed over the years, stemming from an interest in hill walking and the stunning natural environment that Scotland has to offer. I have always been fascinated by geology and geography and by how light interacts and transforms the landscape from season to season and moment to moment. I soon found I was timing my arrival on mountains to coincide with the best of the light, and wanting to linger and enjoy the experience. I quickly developed a real passion for photography.

I have always had an affinity with the panoramic format and find it the most natural way of viewing landscape, complementing the way that we see the world through our own eyes, and I have used it exclusively in this book. I was introduced to this method by the unsurpassed work of Colin Prior, joining a whole generation of photographers who have been inspired by his work and the power of the panoramic format.

My earliest digital images were not taken with a panoramic camera, so I would stitch two or three digital images together. Although this technique can produce the desired effect, it is not without its problems. Barrel distortion, exposure matching, parallax error and imprecise image alignment can all present serious challenges to the overall quality of images created in this way.

I have therefore gone in the opposite direction from most by moving from digital photography to film cameras. I feel that film provides the most authentic record of the landscape, while the limited (and expensive) number of shots available focuses the mind and imposes a more disciplined approach on planning and composition. The use of film also precludes the temptation to digitally manipulate images. The use of imaging software is not necessarily a bad thing but I believe the landscape photographer has an underlying responsibility to preserve as much authenticity as possible, conveying the essence of an image as it was actually shot and experienced.

ACKNOWLEDGMENTS

I would like to thank all the people who have directly helped me with the production of this book. Above all my good friend Colin Marshall, who helped from the very start of this project and has tirelessly assisted with the text and final image selection. A special mention too for my wife, Alison, who accompanied me on many excursions north, often at short notice and always without question. Alison has also stood by my side for many of the images you see within this book and I will always be in debt to her for her support, understanding and patience while waiting for me waiting for the light! Thanks also to Ian Rodney, who kindly prepared the hand-illustrated map of Scotland, and to Ian Scovell, who provided invaluable advice and an exceptional scanning service, along with David Hall of Blueskyimages, who was also instrumental in supplying a large volume of images. Further thanks to David Morrison, Martin Laycock, George Yule, Dr Gareth Jones, Derek Copland, John Kelly, Scott O'Donnell, my mum and dad and all at Frances Lincoln.

For more information, images, prints and calendars, visit www.landandlight.co.uk